CENTRAL LIBRARY
828 "I" STREET
SACRAMENTO, CA 95814
MAY - - 2004

T2-BQH-381

Your

Travel

Guide to

AMERICA'S OLD WEST

Your

Travel

Guide to

AMERICA'S
OLD WEST

Rita J. Markel

Ŀ LERNER PUBLICATIONS COMPANY • MINNEAPOLIS

To Michael

Copyright © 2004 by Rita J. Markel

All rights reserved. International copyright secured. No part of this book may be reproduced, stored in a retrieval system, or transmitted in any form or by any means—electronic, mechanical, photocopying, recording, or otherwise—without the prior written permission of Lerner Publications Company, except for the inclusion of brief quotations in an acknowledged review.

Lerner Publications Company
A division of Lerner Publishing Group
241 First Avenue North
Minneapolis, MN 55401 U.S.A.

Website address: www.lernerbooks.com

Library of Congress Cataloging-in-Publication Data

Markel, Rita J.
    Your travel guide to America's Old West / by Rita J. Markel.
        p.   cm. — (Passport to history)
    Summary: Takes readers on a journey back in time in order to experience life in the American West in the 1800s, describing clothing, accommodations, foods, local customs, transportation, a few notable personalities, and more. Includes bibliographical references and index.
    ISBN: 0–8225–3074–0 (lib. bdg. : alk. paper)
    1. West (U.S.)—Description and travel—Juvenile literature. 2. West (U.S.)—Social life and customs—19th century—Juvenile literature. 3. Frontier and pioneer life—West (U.S.)—Juvenile literature. 4. West (U.S.)—Guidebooks—Juvenile literature. [1. West (U.S.)—Description and travel. 2. West (U.S.)—Social life and customs—19th century. 3. Frontier and pioneer life—West (U.S.)] I. Title. II. Passport to history (Minneapolis, Minn.)
F591.Y66 2004
917.604'44—dc21   2003005620

Manufactured in the United States of America
1 2 3 4 5 6 – JR – 09 08 07 06 05 04

CONTENTS

INTRODUCTION

GETTING STARTED

Welcome to Passport to History. You will be traveling through time and space to America's Old West of the nineteenth century. This vast area stretches from the Mississippi River to the Pacific Ocean. Your trip will take you across the Great Plains, over the snowcapped Rocky Mountains, into the desert Southwest, and to the magnificent Pacific Coast. As you plan your trip, this handy guide will help you every step of the way. It will answer questions such as:

- ➤ **Where should I stay?**
- ➤ **What should I see?**
- ➤ **Who should I meet during my visit?**
- ➤ **Which way to the gold?**

Remember, you are going back in time to an unfamiliar culture. Some of the things you would take along on an ordinary trip didn't exist during this time period. So leave your boom box behind. No cell phones. No sleeping bag or mosquito repellant, either. The Old West isn't known for its comforts. But don't worry. The locals do just fine without all these modern conveniences, and with a little help from this book, you will too.

Covered wagons and horse-drawn carts loaded with supplies make their way through the streets of Helena, Montana, a frontier town.

NOTE TO THE TRAVELER

Some of the information in this guide comes from eyewitness accounts written by people who lived in the Old West. They recorded their experiences in letters, diaries, and newspapers. But historians and other experts look at additional sources, as well. They study maps, dwellings, pottery, tools, and other objects people left behind. They also study paintings, photographs, and government documents. From all these sources, they form ideas about what everyday life was like in the Old

West. By traveling back through time, you might see some things the experts didn't notice. And your conclusions about the West might be quite different from theirs.

WHY VISIT THE OLD WEST?

There's a lot of ground to cover in the Old West. You won't be able to see everything on your trip. But you will see some of the people and places that made the West famous. You'll see farmers and ranchers working the land, cowboys and their herds, and miners looking for that big gold or silver strike. You'll see Mormon pioneers seeking religious freedom, and gamblers and hustlers looking for fools.

You'll want to meet the Native Americans for sure. They were the first settlers, arriving thousands of years before everyone else. Native Americans, also called Indians, are divided into about two hundred different

AMERICA'S
OLD WEST

N

| 0 | 100 | 200 | 300 | |
in miles
| 0 | 200 | 400 | |
in kilometers

groups, called tribes. Each tribe has its own lifestyle and customs.

Mexican Americans live in the Old West too. In fact, until the mid-nineteenth century, much of the American West is Mexican territory. Mexican Americans are descended from Spanish explorers and settlers, so they mainly speak Spanish. You're likely to meet Mexican Americans any place you go in what is the modern-day American Southwest. Some of them live on huge farms and ranches.

You'll see people of other backgrounds in the West, as well. You'll meet African Americans fleeing slavery or its memories. You'll see immigrants—people who have come to America from other countries. Many Chinese immigrants also live in the Old West.

Many people in the Old West come from the East Coast of the United States. The settlers usually come by wagon, traveling along one of several trails that lead west. The most famous route is the Oregon Trail. The travelers from the East are called emigrants.

In your travels through the Old West, you may see things that disturb you. But you will also see things that fascinate and delight you. You will see beauty and excitement. You will see a wealth of natural resources, landscapes, and cultures. For some, the West is a place of loss and difficulty. For others, it is a place of hope and opportunity. You'll see all of this—and more—on your trip to America's Old West.

Now Hear This

"It was all so beautiful—the red rock, the green fields . . . the mighty mountains, the rugged cedars and sage-brush spicing up the warm air."

—*Wyoming settler Elinore Pruitt Stewart*

THE BASICS

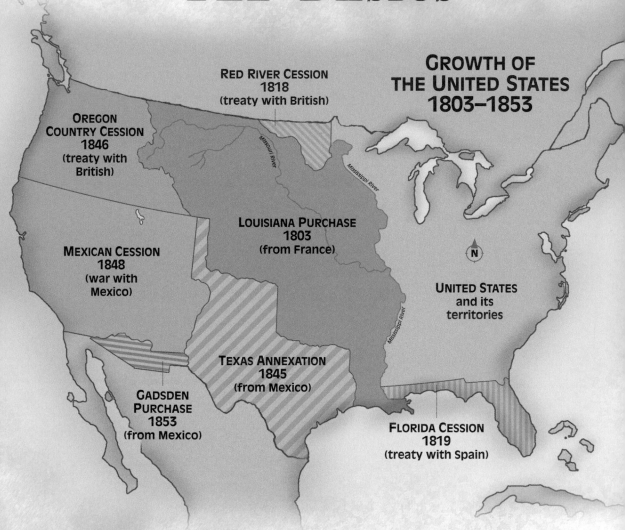

RED RIVER CESSION
1818
(treaty with British)

GROWTH OF
THE UNITED STATES
1803–1853

OREGON
COUNTRY CESSION
1846
(treaty with
British)

Missouri River

Mississippi River

LOUISIANA PURCHASE
1803
(from France)

MEXICAN CESSION
1848
(war with
Mexico)

N

UNITED STATES
and its
territories

Mississippi River

GADSDEN
PURCHASE
1853
(from Mexico)

TEXAS ANNEXATION
1845
(from Mexico)

FLORIDA CESSION
1819
(treaty with Spain)

The United States more than doubled in size in the 1800s due to large land acquisitions.

LOCATION LOWDOWN

Don't look for the Old West in one place. You will have trouble finding it. Western borders change many times during the 1800s.

The first change comes in 1803, when President Thomas Jefferson makes the Louisiana Purchase. This real estate deal is one of the best buys in history. For about $15 million, France sells the United States a giant piece of land—827,987 square miles, to be exact. That's about three cents an acre! This purchase extends the western frontier of the United

States from the Mississippi River to the Rocky Mountains. West of the purchase is Oregon Country, which is claimed by both Great Britain and the United States. In 1846 the two nations split the territory north and south at the Canadian border.

South of Oregon Country is a huge chunk of territory that belongs to Mexico. This includes the present-day state of California and most of the American Southwest. The United States makes its position clear: it wants all this land and is willing to fight for it. Some Americans don't wait for war or agreements. They head west, long before the country's official boundaries change. Mexico stands firm, and the Mexican War (1846–1848) begins. By the end of the war, Texas, California, and much of the Southwest belong to the United States. Congress buys more land from Mexico in 1853.

WHEN TO VISIT

Except for a small number of trappers and fur traders, few white Americans enter the western frontier before 1804. That's the year President Jefferson sends Meriwether Lewis and William Clark to check things out. They and their men, known as the Corps of Discovery, leave from St. Louis, in modern-day Missouri. They head northwest through the Louisiana Purchase and Oregon Country. Eventually, the corps has thirty-three members, including William Clark's African American slave, York, and a young Native American woman named Sacagawea. She becomes the expedition's unofficial guide.

Meriwether Lewis and William Clark (center) *traveled about eight thousand miles in two and one-half years to map and explore the West. Sacagawea is pictured at right.*

Cowboys drove large herds of cattle through the dry expanses of the West.

The corps's job is to lay boundaries for the territory gained by the Louisiana Purchase and to find an easy passage to the Pacific Ocean. Two and one-half years later, the explorers return with maps of vast, unsettled lands, rich with plant and animal life. They have found a passage to the Pacific, but it isn't an easy one. To reach the ocean, the travelers have to cross steep mountains, fast-moving rivers, and treacherous deserts. At times they nearly die from hunger or extreme heat or cold. They also meet some unfriendly native people. Other expeditions follow, and more maps are made. More Americans grow eager to move west.

By the 1820s, white Americans have started ranching in Texas. By the 1830s, they've established towns and farms just west of the Mississippi River. By the 1840s, you can team up with an emigrant family traveling the Oregon Trail. They're headed for the rich farmland and mild climate beyond the Rockies. Of the several trails that lead west, the Oregon Trail is most heavily traveled. Experts estimate that between 350,000 and 500,000 people took the trail west, most of them between 1843 and the 1870s. After the Civil War (1861–1865), you can visit one of the many farming families who hurry to the Great Plains to claim land that the government has opened for settlement.

The California gold rush begins in 1848. In 1849 some 30,000 gold seekers jam the trails west to California. By the end of that year, as many

Hot Hint

After falling behind the other wagons in their train, the Donner Party, heading west in 1846, gets trapped by mountain snows. Only forty-seven of the original eighty-one people in the party survive, some by eating the bodies of the dead. One survivor, a child named Virginia Reed, warns future emigrants, "Never take no cutoffs [short cuts] and [hurry] along as fast as you can."

as 90,000 adventurers from all over the world, including children and teens, have arrived to try their luck. Many miners are Chinese, African American, Mexican American, or Native American. Cities develop wherever the miners go. New businesses such as banking, mail and freight services, and mining-supply outfits grow and prosper. There are big silver strikes too. Between 1859 and 1865, huge deposits of silver—and gold—are taken from the Comstock Lode, near Virginia City, Nevada.

You may get a chance to see the Pony Express, but you'll have to be quick. This delivery service has a short life—April 3, 1860, to November 20, 1861. Its legendary, hard-riding, young horsemen carry mail to western towns and

Prospectors pan for gold.

cities at breakneck speeds. But in October 1861, a company called Western Union begins sending nearly instant transcontinental telegraph messages over electric wires. That's the end of the Pony Express.

The heyday of the American cowboy is 1865 to 1880. To experience the cowboy's life, you won't find a better place than Texas. From there you can catch a cattle drive on the famous Chisholm Trail or Dodge City Trail. The busiest year is 1871, when cowboys drive six hundred thousand cattle along the trails to market.

WHOSE LAND IS THIS ANYWAY?

When you're in the West, you may wonder who owns the land. Native Americans have been living here the longest. They've established tribal homelands and hunting grounds. At times Native American tribes have gone to war with one another to gain or defend territory. And many want to fight the United States to keep the emigrants out. Native Americans are skilled at living off the land, but they do not think that anyone can *own* the land, just as no one can own the sun or the moon.

The U.S. government believes it can—and does—own the West. It has either fought or paid European nations and Mexico for much of the land. The government promises to set aside some land for Native Americans. But it also encourages hordes of emigrants to settle in the

West. Under the 1862 Homestead Act, the government gives free land to settlers. It also gives large amounts of prime western land to railroad companies. It eventually allows settlers, miners, and ranchers to move onto lands that have been set aside for Native Americans.

To defend its new territory, the government sets up army posts and forts throughout the West. At times, misunderstandings, broken promises, and bad will result in violence between native warriors and the U.S. Army or between natives and settlers. The army also deliberately goes on the attack, waging a series of campaigns to defeat the Indians. Although native people throughout the West fight hard to keep their lands, the surviving tribes end up confined to reserved areas, or reservations.

SIDE TRIP TRIVIA

Native Americans use the moon as a calendar. The crescent of a new moon marks each new month. The Arapaho people call April "the moon of ice breaking on the river." The Sioux call October "the moon of falling leaves" and December "the moon of frost in the tepees." Native people also use the moon to measure distance. If something is "two moons away," it will take about two months to get there.

A group of tepees, homes used by Native Americans of the Great Plains region, lines the horizon.

Native American students at a boarding school run by whites in Nebraska

Some white Americans defend the rights of the native people. However, many whites believe that Native Americans should live like white Americans. Religious teachers, called missionaries, try to convert some tribes to Christianity. They send native children away from their families to attend school. There, the children lose their cultural identities. They learn to speak English and to dress, talk, and even think like white Americans.

SAY WHAT?

Emigrants coming from the East speak mainly English, but Spanish also comes in handy when you're traveling into the West, especially in cowboy country. On the range, Mexican cowboys use Spanish words such as *vaquero* (cowboy) and *lazo* (lasso, *pictured at left*).

Talking to the Native Americans in their own languages is tricky. Native people belong to many different cultural groups. The language of one group is usually unrelated to the language of others. Some native people—especially on the Great Plains—use sign language, or hand gestures, to communicate with those from other tribes. Like the settlers and other newcomers, you might find sign language useful.

Native Americans and Mexicans have already named most places in the West by the time Lewis and Clark arrive. Some of the original names stick. Examples include Albuquerque in modern-day New Mexico, named for a Spanish duke. Kamiah, a town in modern-day Idaho, is named for a Nez Perce Indian word meaning "rope." There is a catch, though. The names can be hard to spell and pronounce. To get names right, ask a local. You'll be in for a few surprises.

Lewis and Clark often don't know the old Spanish and Indian names. So they make up their own names to identify places they draw on their maps. They name many places after members of their expedition. For instance, they name the Sacagawea River after their guide Sacagawea. They name a large rock formation, Pompey's Pillar, for her infant son, Pompey. Both the river and the pillar are in present-day Montana.

Handy WORDS & PHRASES

Some of the first Europeans to explore North America were French. When they saw the vast grasslands of the Great Plains, they gave them the name *prairie*. This word is French for "large meadow."

WHICH CITIES TO VISIT

INDEPENDENCE, MISSOURI

Most emigrants coming from the East pick up the Oregon Trail at a town along the Missouri River. Independence is the most popular of these "jumping off" towns, so it's a good place to hitch a ride on a wagon going west.

Mingle with the crowds and watch how they organize into groups for the trip, make ground rules, and choose leaders. Carpenters hammer almost nonstop as they hurry to finish wagons ordered by emigrants. Loud clanging comes from sheds as blacksmiths forge wheels and tools.

A family of four may need more than one thousand dollars for the trip. Many emigrants raise this cash by selling their farms back east. Much of the money is spent right in Independence, where people scurry to buy supplies. Store shelves empty fast, making the merchants very happy—and very rich!

Food for a family of four, plus tools, cooking implements, and clothing, can weigh two thousand pounds. All that plus a wagon will be pulled by animals—usually four or six oxen. Guidebooks warn emigrants to take only the essentials, but everybody sneaks something they shouldn't into their wagons. You'll notice plenty of furniture and other luxuries along the trail. These get tossed out when the trail gets rough

and the animals tire. So don't even consider bringing your souvenir cannonball from the Revolutionary War. Same goes for cast-iron stoves.

NICODEMUS, KANSAS

Stop off in Nicodemus, Kansas, the West's first all-black community. It is founded in 1877 by "Exodusters," African Americans who have fled the South after the Civil War. Former slaves, the Exodusters take their name from the Bible's Book of Exodus, which tells how the ancient Hebrews fled slavery in Egypt for a new, free life in Israel.

The Exodusters get reports that Nicodemus has rich soil and plentiful water. But when they arrive, they find dry, almost treeless prairie. They have little money and few farm tools. More than 130 families come

TAKE IT from a Local

"I looked with all the eyes I had. . . . Where is Nicodemus? I don't see it. . . . The scenery to me was not at all inviting. I began to cry."

—Williana Hickman,
on seeing the Kansas land her family had bought

Although reports of fertile lands in Nicodemus, Kansas, prove false, African Americans who move there make the most of their new home, free from slavery.

to Nicodemus in 1877, but 60 families immediately return to the South. Living in caves they dig out of the hills, the others nearly starve their first winter. But they stay in Nicodemus and work to build their community. If you walk through the town after 1881, you'll find churches, schools, two newspaper offices, and other businesses.

SALT LAKE CITY, UTAH

This is a city built on faith, hard work—and murder. It is founded by Brigham Young and twelve thousand followers of the Church of Jesus Christ of Latter-Day Saints, commonly known as Mormons. The church gets its start back east. In the 1830s, angry mobs, opposed to the church's teachings, kill some of its members in Missouri. In 1844 mobs in Illinois shoot and kill the church's founder, Joseph Smith. Church members know it is time to go west.

The group takes the Oregon Trail over the Rocky Mountains to Fort Bridger in Wyoming. They then head southwest, into an area so barren and dry that no other settlers want it. Near the banks of the Great Salt

Mormon pioneers break for camp on their long journey west to Salt Lake City.

Now Hear This

"A broad and barren plain . . . blistering on the rays of the midsummer sun . . . the paradise of the lizard, the cricket, and the rattlesnake."

— A Mormon pioneer describing the future site of Salt Lake City.

Lake, they found their town in 1847. They begin planning the city's design, digging irrigation ditches, and planting crops the first day they arrive.

If you visit after 1867, you'll see the newly built tabernacle, where church members gather for choir. You'll notice that all the streets lead out from there in an orderly, gridlike manner. For fun, jump into the Great Salt Lake. Its briny water is twice as salty as the ocean. Because of all the salt, you won't sink.

SAN ANTONIO, TEXAS

This is an old town. It was first home to Native Americans, who called it Yanaguana. In the sixteenth century, Spanish explorers came looking for gold and other treasures to bring back to Spain. In 1718 the Spanish renamed the town San Antonio. They built a mission, or church compound, here. Called the Alamo, the mission has thick walls, which make it a strong fort as well as a church.

In 1836 it is here that Texas rebels and their American sympathizers, including James Bowie and Davy Crocket, fight bravely against overwhelming odds to free Texas from Mexican control. All of the rebels are killed. But later that year, Texas does win independence from Mexico. In 1845 Texas joins the United States.

IMPORTANT Safety Tip

Stay out of downtown San Antonio between February 23 and March 6, 1836. You could get caught in the crossfire between Texas rebels and General Santa Anna's Mexican troops.

Many San Antonio residents speak both English and Spanish. After 1860 you will also hear a lot of "cow talk." The town is a favorite stopping place for cowboys as they drive their cattle on the trails to Kansas.

SAN FRANCISCO, CALIFORNIA

Chinese immigrants call the United States Gum San, or Golden Mountain. You'll find out why if you visit San Francisco. You'll get the *mountain* part as soon as you start—gasp!—climbing the series of steep hills the city is built on. The *golden* part comes during the gold rush of 1848 and 1849.

If you visit during the gold rush years, watch out. You risk being trampled by miners stampeding into the city from all around the world. They're headed for Sutter's Mill, about one hundred miles northeast of San Francisco, where gold has just been discovered. Not everyone finds gold, but those who do often come back to San Francisco to spend their loot. San Franciscans get rich by selling miners supplies, filing their land claims, and handling their gold. The city soon becomes the financial center of the West.

An artist's rendition of early San Francisco pictures dwellings built on the area's hillsides.

Because of the gold rush, San Francisco grows in population, from nine hundred to twenty-five thousand people in just one year. By 1851 it has fifteen fire companies, three hospitals, eighteen churches—and 537 saloons. It also has more than two dozen newspapers, some written in Chinese for the city's many Chinese residents.

You might wait until 1873 to visit San Francisco. Then you can ride a cable car instead of walking up the steep hills. Take the car to the top of Nob Hill, where the newly rich have built their mansions.

Then check out Chinatown, near the center of the city. For safety and a sense of community, the Chinese in San Francisco cluster together. Many folks here wear China's traditional clothing: a black tunic over loose-fitting black pants. The men and boys often wear their hair in a long braid. There's a lot to see: Chinese restaurants, laundries, food markets, drugstores, and other shops. A walk through this crowded neighborhood will give you some of the sounds, sights, and smells of China.

Back TO THE FUTURE

Levi Strauss and Company, one of the world's most famous clothing manufacturers, got its start in San Francisco. The company made denim work pants and jackets for miners and cowboys.

MONEY MATTERS

A necklace made of shell and stone beads would have been traded for other goods in the Old West.

A WOLF SCALP FOR YOUR THOUGHTS

The surest way to get what you need in the West is to have something to trade. Native Americans often trade buffalo hides or strings of shells or beads. Beaver pelts and wolf scalps are also excellent trading items. Milk and eggs are always in demand, as are bullets, tobacco, and horses. In gold-mining areas such as Sacramento, California, and Last Chance Gulch, Montana, gold dust and gold nuggets are accepted as cash. Some Americans establish trading posts in the West in the 1840s. Local Native Americans and emigrants shop at the posts.

A gold nugget

MONEY TALKS

Coins are commonly used in the West. Examples are the ten-dollar gold piece, known as an eagle, and the twenty-dollar gold piece, or double eagle. Half and quarter eagles, as well as silver dollars, are also used out west. Up until 1857, when the U.S. government bans all foreign coins, you can use the Spanish real, known as a bit. A bit is worth twelve and one-half cents.

How much money should you bring? That depends on where you go, when you go, and what you want. In the 1860s, the stagecoach fare from Salt Lake City, Utah, to Atchison, Kansas, costs $150. A third-class boat ticket from San Francisco to New York City costs $135. A seat for a concert in Lincoln, Nebraska, costs fifty cents in 1869. In 1874 Doc Holliday pulls teeth for $3 a pop in Dallas, Texas.

A WORKING WAGE

Monthly salaries in the West depend on the year, the location, and the demand for a worker's skills. In the 1850s, a rookie cowboy may earn anything from just food and housing to $14 a month. But when the price of cattle is high, an experienced cowboy can get $120 a month. In 1880 a California farmworker makes $70 a month. During the same era, an enlisted man in the U.S. Army earns just $13 each month, with a bed and food thrown in. Officers do better—$116 to $290 a month—but they must buy their own food.

Prices
OF COMMON GOODS

A pair of moccasins: $1 (1847)

Letter delivery via the Pony Express: $5 (1860–1861)

A sturdy buffalo robe: $7 (1863)

One pound of cheese: 12¢ (1863)

A steak in a San Francisco restaurant: 50¢ (1875)

How to Get Around

Native Americans of the Great Plains ride on horseback.

By Land

Once you're in the West, a great way to travel is by horse. The Spanish brought horses to North and South America in the sixteenth century. Within one hundred years, many Native Americans were using horses in their daily lives. Horses allow Native Americans to travel far, trade with distant tribes, and follow buffalo and other game. Some native warriors fight on horseback.

Some native people are skillful horse breeders, and most native tribes have a few horses they're willing to trade or sell. The Nez Perce in Oregon Country breed Appaloosas, sturdy horses that are highly prized in the West.

Native people also travel on foot. They have used the same trails for centuries, creating a vast network of pathways across North America. American emigrants will follow some of these trails as well.

If you're traveling with the wagon trains, the Oregon Trail is your best bet. After you cross the Rocky Mountains, you'll find secondary trails branching off to California and Utah. A less popular option is the Santa Fe Trail, which leads from Missouri into the Southwest, with two branches, the Gila Trail and the Old Spanish Trail, to southern California.

Time is critical on the wagon trip west. If the emigrants set out too early in spring, there won't be enough grass on the prairies to feed the livestock. If they start too late, they may not make it through the mountains before the heavy snowfalls. As they travel, they watch carefully for

A wagon train crosses a steep mountain trail in the Rockies.

27

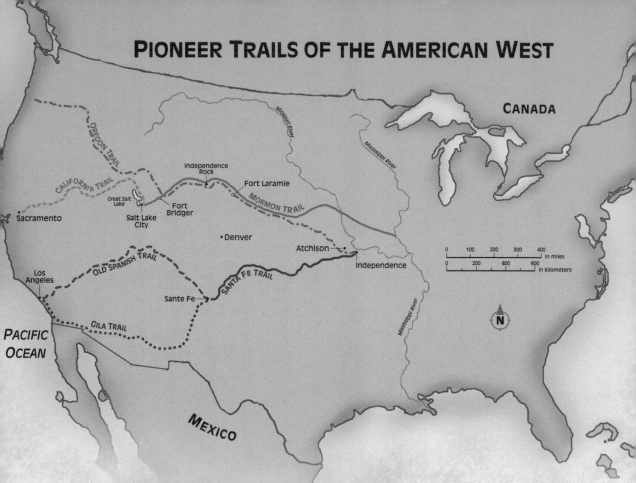

PIONEER TRAILS OF THE AMERICAN WEST

important landmarks. If they reach Independence Rock near Fort Laramie in Wyoming Territory by July 4, they know they're on schedule.

The trails west have one thing in common: they're all bad. Slowed by deep ruts, rocks, fallen trees, and frequent and dangerous river crossings, the early wagon trains take up to six months to get from Missouri to Oregon Country. After many years of heavy traffic, the trails are worn smoother, with fewer obstacles blocking the path. Smart businesspeople eventually build bridges or run ferryboats across dangerous rivers. Emigrants willingly pay fees to get their wagons across safely. With these improvements, a wagon train can get to Oregon Country in three months.

Even though they're slow, oxen generally pull wagons on the trails. They're stronger and more obedient than horses or mules, and they adjust well to a diet of prairie grasses. The ideal setup for an emigrant family? A team of six oxen, yoked in pairs. A mule is a good choice for gold miners, who want to get where they're going fast. Mules can't pull as much as oxen, but miners travel pretty light.

If an emigrant family has a horse, one family member will ride horseback alongside the wagon. Riding in the wagon itself is a tooth-rattling

Get ready for crowded conditions if you travel by stagecoach. Every inch of space is used.

experience and only increases the weight the animals must pull. So most folks walk, covering fifteen to twenty miles a day.

As early as 1849, stagecoaches run between western cities and also carry travelers coming from the East. If you're traveling light and don't mind close contact with strangers, this is the ride for you. Count on only fifteen inches of bench space per person if the coach is full. Unless you can sleep sitting bolt upright, avoid the middle bench (it has no back). Coaches travel around the clock, with short stops to change horses or drivers. The average speed is eight miles per hour. Fully loaded, stagecoaches can carry twenty-one passengers: nine inside and twelve on top. It'll take about eight days to get from Atchison, Kansas, to Denver, Colorado. Same trip by wagon train? Five weeks. Beware: Stagecoaches carry gold and silver, cash, and other valuables. Stagecoach robberies are common.

Now Hear This

"Wanted . . . young, skinny, wiry fellows . . . not over eighteen. Must be expert riders, willing to risk death daily. Orphans preferred."

—*Want ad for Pony Express riders*

IMPORTANT
Safety Tip

In 1874 Joseph F. Glidden sells a wire that can be used as fencing in areas where wood is scarce, such as the Great Plains. While traveling by foot or horse, avoid barbed wire if you can. The sharp, thornlike "barbs" twisted at intervals into the wire are meant to keep livestock in and unwelcome guests out.

During the 1850s, stagecoaches, pack mules, and wagons carry mail between the eastern states and the West. Then comes the Pony Express, staffed by young men riding seventy-five miles a day across rough and dangerous territory. This system cuts the time of mail delivery between Missouri and California from three weeks to less than ten days. But the telegraph puts the Pony Express out of business in late 1861.

The transcontinental railway is completed in 1869. It links the country from coast to coast. The western segment of the railway is laid

The transcontinental railway brings passengers to a small frontier town.

almost entirely by Chinese men. They work hard for low pay. Skilled in the use of explosives, such as nitroglycerin, they perform the dangerous job of blasting tunnels through mountains. Railroad workers have another name for nitroglycerin. They call it "bang juice." After the railway is complete, you can travel from Omaha, Nebraska, to Sacramento, California, in just four days—if you can pony up the one hundred dollars for first-class train fare. If not, third-class trains charge only forty dollars. But they're hitched to the back of slower freight trains and will get you to Sacramento in about ten days.

Back TO THE FUTURE

Railroads arrange for Chinese laborers to come to America and build the transcontinental railroad. But some Americans think railroad and other construction jobs should go to white workers. So in 1882, the United States passes the Chinese Exclusion Act, banning Chinese immigrants. The law stays in effect until 1943.

Native Americans in San Francisco fish the ocean waters in a canoe.

Got gold fever? In a hurry? You can take a ship south along the Atlantic coast to the Isthmus of Panama, a small strip of land in Central America. Cross the isthmus by donkey and canoe. Hopefully, you won't catch a deadly disease in the jungle. Then sail up the Pacific coast to San Francisco. If you're lucky, you'll save a few months of travel time this way.

Some folks bypass Panama and sail around Cape Horn at the tip of South America. It's a thirteen-thousand-mile trip that will take six months, but you'll never forget this experience. The ships sail through some of the roughest water in the world. Most passengers get seasick. Don't slip on the vomit. It's everywhere.

Local Customs
& Manners

What You Can Expect from the Locals

When you're visiting local folks, travel smart. Learn a little about the people you meet. And always be ready for the unexpected. You'll find that most westerners love visitors, especially when they bring news, gossip, and trade goods. Distances are great between western villages and settlements, so many people long for human contact. Make it clear that you don't plan to take your hosts' land, jump their claim, steal their livestock, or interfere with their water supply, and most people will make you feel welcome. To get invited back, show that you are fair, willing to work, and, above all, optimistic.

Although this frontier family may not look friendly, most Westerners welcome visitors.

In your travels, you will see that native cultures can differ greatly from one another. If you visit the Pueblo people in the Southwest, for instance, you'll meet farmers. They live in ancient high-rise buildings and never travel far beyond their homes. They fight only when attacked and believe it is wrong to kill another person—even in battle. If you stay with the Sioux, you'll watch them chase buffalo across the plains. You'll be on the move constantly, taking along your home, a collapsible tepee. If the tribe goes to war, you'll see them honor their warriors for killing the enemy.

You are likely to see African Americans wherever you go in the West. If you're in cattle country around 1870, you'll find that many cowboys working the range are black—probably one in four. At times you'll see people treated unfairly because of their race. For example, African American emigrants may be asked to follow a wagon train at a distance. They aren't allowed to travel alongside the white families in the train. Unfair treatment isn't reserved just for blacks. Chinese, non-English-speaking Europeans, Mexican Americans, Native Americans, and people of any mixed race often face unfair laws and practices—even brutality.

African American cowboys pose for a photo.

The Becker sisters team up to brand cattle on their ranch in San Luis Valley, Colorado.

Don't be surprised if you see women branding cattle, digging for gold, or driving stagecoaches in the West. Western women are tough and adventurous. They can vote in elections too—long before women in the East earn that right. But women are in short supply in some parts of the West, especially in mining areas and cattle country. Lonely men have a hard time finding wives. They sometimes resort to choosing brides from mail-order companies, often from overseas. Other men place ads in newspapers, stating the traits they'd like in a wife. Mexican American, Native American, and certain European parents may arrange marriages for their children. Girls are sometimes promised in marriage by age thirteen. But, in general, Western women marry when they are much older.

An Apache bride wears a traditional wedding costume.

Native Americans of the Pacific Northwest were expert fishers.

FROM DAWN TO DUSK

Daily life is hard in the West. There is always work to be done, so be ready to join in. In the Pacific Northwest, you can help Native Americans gather salmon. They'll teach you how to catch fish using nets, hooks, or just a spear. Be realistic. It may take a while to catch fish this way.

Head into the Southwest and find a Pueblo village, where you can help the men as they harvest corn. Don't care for yellow corn? How about red, white, black, blue, pink, or speckled?

Native folks who eat wild game, especially buffalo, are on the road a lot, following the herds. So you'll have to catch up with them. You'll almost certainly be in the way during a buffalo hunt, which is dangerous and requires great skill from the hunter and his horse. Don't worry. You can always help at the campsite by putting up or taking down the tepee. This job is done by the women of the tribe, with a little help from the kids. A tepee consists of a buffalo-hide cover and supporting poles. The cover alone weighs about 150 pounds. But the women can put a tepee up and take it down almost as easily as an umbrella.

A buffalo hunt is an exciting and dangerous event!

When you travel the Oregon Trail, be ready for discomfort. Temperatures on the Great Plains routinely top one hundred degrees. In desert areas, there is never enough water to drink. In the mountains, the animals must be coaxed to pull heavy loads up steep inclines. Going down the other side is worse. Sometimes it's impossible to brake the heavy wagons on the way down, so you may have to help lower them with ropes. You will be crossing and recrossing rivers and streams that are often deep and swift. The water is so cold it makes your bones ache.

KIDS' STUFF

You'll see lots of children everywhere you go in the West. On the trail, children are expected to keep up with the wagons and help out. They must gather fuel for campfires. On the prairies, there are few trees but lots of buffalo. Dried buffalo droppings can be burned like wood. The bigger the "buffalo chip" the better. A flat one can be tossed like a Frisbee. Make sure it's good and dry, though.

If you visit a settler farm, you'll find four-year-olds hauling water, breaking sod, chopping wood, and watching younger children. Boys as young as seven hunt game with the family rifle. Children of all ages help

Even the youngest children have chores in the Old West. This young girl feeds the chickens.

keep frontier homes free of pesky flies in summer. Long, sticky streams of flypaper hang in every room, but some flies don't stick. Good fly-bashing skills are a must.

Many settler children attend school, but only when they're not needed to work at home. School calendars are set according to planting and harvesting seasons. Don't expect bright, clean classrooms, though. Most settler schools are simple one-room buildings. Some are no more than flimsy sheds. And unless you bring a box along to sit on, you may have to stand up all day.

One challenge for teachers is keeping the students out of the out-house, or outdoor toilet. Sometimes called the "not so nice," this is a very popular place. It seats two comfortably and often provides fascinating toilet paper—pages from mail-order catalogs, with lots of pictures of things to buy.

Native children don't go to organized schools, but for them class is al-ways in session. They must learn to use bows and arrows, hunt or gather their food, and build their dwellings. There are no set times for learning

Students and their teacher (back right) *pose outside their sod schoolhouse.*

these survival skills—and no hard chairs to sit on. The teachers? The most skilled adults in the village.

Despite all the work and study, western children still find ways to have fun. Fore example, they make toys out of whatever they have. They make dolls out of corn husks, scraps of cloth, or deerskin. Nez Perce children play flipper. The object of the game? To hit your opponent with a mud ball, flipped off the flattened end of a stick.

LOCAL MANNERS

Standards of behavior vary widely in the West. In some towns, it's against the law to hang your laundry out to dry on a Sunday (although enforcement is unlikely). In other places, teachers are supposed to attend church regularly and read the Bible after finishing a ten-hour workday at school.

Western parents make lots of rules for children. "Elbows off the table!" is a common command at mealtime. Thumb-suckers must wear mittens year-round. Children learn about morals from books by Parson

Gambling, lying, and swearing will get you a lashing at school. In Sacramento, California, the punishment for climbing trees is calculated by the foot. The higher you climb, the bigger the penalty.

Weems. His popular stories relate the good deeds of heroic figures in American history, such as President George Washington. In school, teachers are allowed to strike, or lash, misbehaving children with a whip or a stick.

Standards of behavior slip considerably in mining camps and cattle towns. In rough places like Tombstone, Arizona, almost all socializing is done in saloons and gambling houses. Whiskey is the drink of choice, and nearly everyone has a gun. So watch out for trouble, and don't visit on payday.

This saloon's owner has a sense of humor. The tavern's name is Whiskey the Road to Ruin.

Western men chew and spit tobacco in public. It's not considered rude. Ladies, however, usually chew in private. You might see a spittoon—a round, low container—sitting on the floor in which refined folks spit their tobacco after it becomes juicy. With a little practice and a good eye, male and female spitters can usually hit their target from a pretty fair distance.

WESTWARD—WHEW!

How do you keep clean in the West? A native tribe might use a sweathouse, a dome-shaped hut that seats about six people. By pouring water over hot stones, they get a good steam going. Steam makes you sweat. Scrape the sweat off later, and you're pretty clean.

You can't take a steam bath in a covered wagon, but some folks heading west wouldn't bother to bathe even if they could. A few boast of making the entire trip without taking their clothes off once. A popular 1859 guidebook for emigrants advises taking an extra set of underwear and a few pairs of socks for a three-month journey. Forty-five days is considered a reasonable workout for the first set of underwear.

On the trail, clothing soon stiffens with dirt, sweat, and grease. Along for the ride are little critters called lice. Wading into a stream fully dressed is as close as most emigrants come to bathing. They lie in the sun to get dry. Gold miners are even dirtier. They don't change their bedding for months, and they sleep in their dirty clothes, including their boots. (By the way, the folks back east are not too particular about hygiene, either.)

If you visit a settler, you'll understand why winter baths are *really* unpopular. First, somebody has to lug the water for the bath. This involves many trips to the creek or well. Firing up the stove to heat the water is another big chore. Keeping the water hot in a cold room is impossible. Once you're in the bath, usually a small metal

Hot Hint

Some people chew sprigs of wild mint to take the edge off their bad breath. But, in general, westerners don't worry much about dental care.

tub, soap will sting your eyes and leave your skin feeling slimy. It smells like fat and ashes—because that's exactly what it's made of. (By the way, the water you're sitting in has probably already been used by more important members of the household.)

LOCAL BELIEFS

Most native people in the West feel a sacred bond with the earth. Many believe that the earth is their mother, the source of all life. They honor the earth's great life forces, such as the sun and rivers. Most tribes kill only the animals they need to survive. To use animals carelessly, the natives believe, would upset the earth's balance.

Native Americans often give thanks for the earth's gifts. For example, the Navajo make daily offerings of corn pollen to the earth, the sun, and the water. Many tribes hold special celebrations honoring beans, squash, strawberries, and other foods—especially corn. The doors to many native dwellings face east, so that people can honor the sun as it rises each morning. Natives also believe that plants, animals, places, the dead, and even natural events such as storms have spirits. They honor these spirits through prayer, song, dance, and gifts.

Native American men of the Great Plains perform the Buffalo Dance. Sacred ceremonies are rarely pictured, but some Native American groups allow artist George Catlin to record their images.

Traveling preacher Walter Manning (center) *takes his message on the road.*

Most settlers who come west are Christians. Large towns have permanent churches. But many small settlements don't, so worship services are often held in private homes. Preachers are in short supply in the West. Traveling preachers, called circuit riders, travel on horseback from town to town. Upon arrival, a preacher may hold a camp meeting, or outdoor service, that can last for several days. The meeting is a time for worship—and also for picnics, companionship, and flirting. Attendance is good here.

Catholic missions—built by the Spanish—are found throughout California and the Southwest. These large settlements, which include schools, houses, churches, and farmland, serve Mexican American worshipers as well as conquered Native Americans. Many native people live at the missions and work in the fields. They also study Christian teachings and must abide by church rules. At times Native Americans flee the missions or rebel against mission leaders.

People of other faiths live in the West too. Jewish settlers form synagogues, and Chinese immigrants found Buddhist temples. But their numbers are small compared to those of the Christian settlers.

Mourners watch over platform graves at this Native American burial ground. This type of burial was a Plains Indian tradition.

DEATH AND BEYOND

Indians believe that after death, a spirit takes the place of the human or animal who has died. This spirit may be destructive, bringing bad luck to people or whole tribes. Or the spirit may be helpful, guiding and protecting a warrior or a tribe in battle, for instance. Some tribes believe that taking the scalp of a dead enemy provides protection against that enemy's spirit. Native people usually respect the dead, even the animals they must kill to survive.

Funeral customs vary among tribes. Some native people place a body on a raised platform and leave it there until only the bones remain. Then they move the remains to a sacred burial place. Other natives burn the dead person's body. Some tribes bury bodies, but they do not usually mark the graves.

When a death occurs in a settler's household, the deceased is washed and usually dressed in his or her best clothes. The body is placed in a cool room until burial. Towns and cities have cemeteries. Rural folks generally have a family gravesite on their land.

When a death occurs on the trail, there is no time for long good-byes. Sometimes, emigrants dig a grave directly in the path of oncoming wagons. That way, the wagons will pack down the ground as they pass over the site.

Mexican Americans always place crosses on graves. They remember their dead every fall in a four-day celebration called the Days of the Dead. On this holiday, families bring gifts and flowers to the graves of loved ones. But it is more a time of celebration than of mourning. At night on this holiday, children may dress up like ghosts or skeletons, or paint their faces to look like skulls. Adults give them treats. Sound familiar?

SIDE TRIP TRIVIA

The Oregon Trail qualifies as America's longest cemetery. One in twenty emigrants (possibly more) died along the trail. If the graves of those who died were evenly spaced along the trail, there would be a grave every fifty yards from Missouri to Oregon Country.

These pioneer graves were covered with stones to keep animals from digging them up.

What to Wear

Best Dressed in the West

Don't even try to compete with some native people when it comes to dressing in style. The Cheyenne and other tribes of the Great Plains wear deerskin clothing with fringes. This style not only looks cool (the fringe swings when you move), it also makes the clothing roomier. Women sew beads, shells, or porcupine quills in colorful designs on the garments, sometimes adding pieces of glass or metal. Animals such as wolves and deer and natural forces such as lightening and rainbows are thought to have protective powers. So some tribes paint or bead these images onto clothing. The images are meant to keep the wearer from harm.

The Hopi of the Southwest weave their own cotton for summer wear and wool for cooler weather. Their men and boys often go shirtless in hot weather. Chinook men and boys, who live in the mild climate of the Pacific Northwest, often don't wear much at all. If they get cold, they throw on a robe made from softened cedar bark. Don't be surprised to see a native man wearing a sunshield or visor. These are sensible accessories that protect the eyes from the West's strong sun.

Underwear isn't a big seller among native men. In the coldest climates, men might wear fringed briefs. But the underwear of choice is a loincloth, which looks like a short apron, tied at the back. Native women, especially in the Southwest, may wear simple underdresses.

This dress (facing page), *made of deer hide and decorated with fringe and beadwork, is very fashionable among Native American women of the Great Plains.*

Picnickers in Idaho, wearing their Sunday best, rest after their lunch. Hats are common among men and boys. The youngest boy (center) still wears shorts. His older brothers have switched to long pants. Women and girls usually wear dresses.

IS THAT A FLOUR SACK YOU'RE WEARING?

On the frontier, style is usually secondary. If you want to fit in, make your own clothes from something that's already used. Mattress coverings and flour sacks make good dresses and shirts. That canvas from a covered wagon can be made into shirts, pants, or dresses. Same goes for the tent.

A frontier boy is not considered a man until he switches from shorts to long pants. Ideally, the changeover is made at age thirteen. Shorts require less cloth than pants and have no holes in the knees to be mended, so thrifty mothers delay the change as long as they can. Most boys rebel if kept in short pants past age fifteen, however. Men and boys wear cloth shirts. As they become accustomed to the West, they may switch to shirts made of animal skins. Long drawers, or underpants, button at the waist and tie at the ankle. A one-piece undergarment, called a union suit, is available by mail order in the mid-1890s.

Many settler women try to dress like they did back east. But in the West, long skirts restrict movement, catch on barbed wire, and get dirty

Devices such as Dewey's Invisible Dress Elevator are available in the 1880s. The dress elevator is a pulley system that a pioneer woman can pin to any dress. It allows her to quickly raise the garment's hem to avoid mud, manure, brush, or barbed wire. When the danger has passed, she can lower the hem to its usual length.

around livestock. So all western women come to the same conclusion: clothes have to fit their lifestyle. Some women sew heavy buckshot—small metal pellets—into the hems of their skirts to weight them down against strong winds. Women who work outdoors wear shorter, looser clothing. At times you might see women wearing culottes, bloomers that gather at the ankle, leather leggings, or even pants!

Emigrant girls usually wear shorter versions of their mothers' clothing. They are expected to wear sunbonnets, and many do not like it. Although bonnets offer shade from the intense sun, they also restrict the view. A girl or woman of Mexican descent may wear a colorful fringed scarf. She might wear it to cover her head or shoulders, or tie it around her waist. For church or special occasions, she covers her hair with a lacy, shorter scarf called a *mantilla*.

This cowgirl wears wide-legged pants. Western women broke traditional fashion rules to make life easier on the frontier.

49

Famous painter Frederic Remington captures the look of a Mexican vaquero. Decked out in sombrero and chaps, this cowboy is looking good.

Mexicans set the trend for cowboy wear. Their wide-brimmed hats, called sombreros, keep the sun off their faces and rain off their shoulders. Their serapes, or ponchos, serve as raincoats. To protect their legs as they ride on horseback through brush and cacti, they wear *chaperjos*, or chaps, which are leggings made of animal hide. They attach metal spurs *(right)* to the heels of their boots to tap the horse's sides—a reminder of who's the boss.

A cowboy's hat is the first thing he puts on in the morning and the last to go at night. After 1865 he might choose a Stetson, which has a narrower brim than the sombrero. His leather boots are likely to be the most expensive thing he wears. When riding in the dust kicked up by cattle, most cowboys cover their noses and mouths with bandannas.

The intricate squash-blossom hairstyle sported by Hopi girls signals that they are old enough for marriage.

HAIR HELPERS

Native men and women usually wear their hair long, either straight or braided, sometimes coiled at the neck and held in place with a leather thong. Many men pluck out their facial hair. The men of a few tribes grow mustaches or even beards. When she is seventeen, a Hopi girl gets to wear the traditional "squash blossom" hairstyle. This style means she is ready for marriage. Her hair is parted in the middle and twisted into two round shapes that resemble the blossoms of the squash plant. For special occasions, Native American women sometimes apply a red dye to their heads where the hair is parted. If a native woman has cut her hair short, she is in mourning.

Hot Hint

The Chumash of southern California are known for their shiny hair. Like it? Try rubbing your hair with the gum of the mesquite plant, plus clay. Leave the mixture in for a few days, then rinse.

A father prepares to cut his son's hair with a sharp knife.

Among settlers, almost anybody with a sharp tool can manage a passable haircut. A clean shave is another matter—a straight-edged razor can be dangerous. Many men wear mustaches or full beards since that's easier than shaving. As cities and towns expand in the West, barbershops open for business and do well. Customers know that the water will be hot, the razor will be held in a steady hand, and the gossip will be good. A Chinese man may shave most of his head, but he will still grow a long braid in the back. (The emperor will not allow him to reenter China without it.)

Most frontier women wear their hair long, almost always braided or twisted and pinned up on top of their heads. In cities, such as San Francisco and Denver, styles are a bit more imaginative. Urban ladies often curl their hair or fill out their own locks with hairpieces.

BEAUTY BOOSTERS

In rural areas, the use of cosmetics is strongly discouraged. Rouge and lipstick—called "paint"—are said to contain harmful chemicals. Even worse, women who work in saloons and music halls wear cosmetics—

and these ladies have bad reputations. A proper frontier woman might buy a hair- or skin-care product from a traveling peddler. She might use homemade lotions to soften the skin or discourage freckles.

Rural women sometimes wear ribbons in their hair or pinned to a blouse. They wear minimal jewelry—perhaps a wedding ring, a locket, a modest pin, or earrings. Jewelry is more common in big cities. For wealthy ladies, especially *newly* wealthy ladies, the more jewelry the better. Necklaces, rings, bracelets—whatever you've got, wear it!

Among Native Americans, adornments have special meanings. For instance, before going into battle, a warrior paints symbols on his body and horse that identify him as a dangerous opponent. The image of a palm of a hand means the warrior has killed a man in battle. On the Great Plains, warriors wear headdresses decorated with feathers. A feather with a red spot means the warrior has killed an enemy in battle. A feather split down the middle means he has suffered many battle wounds. Many feathers mean many battles.

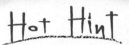

Hot Hint

The eagle represents courage for the Plains tribes, and their warriors use only eagle feathers for their headdresses. The tribes raise their own eagles for the feathers.

Elder Sioux tribe members wear gorgeous feather headdresses and traditional clothing, while a younger member has adopted the cowboy style of dress.

What to See & Do

Medicine Shows

Nowhere in the West will you find better theater than at a traveling medicine show. These shows are very popular in the mid- to late nineteenth century. Go early and try to get up front. Prepare to be cured of all ailments, real or imaginary. You will meet people like Colonel T. A. Edwards, part circus performer, part military man, and a born liar. His product, Ka-Ton-Ka, will cure whatever illness you've got. Like many other medicine salesmen, Edwards swears that his liquid cure-all is made from a secret Native American formula. And it's in short supply, so buy now!

Shows like Edwards's often begin with a parade, leading to a tent or stage. Performers might then play musical instruments, sing, dance, or imitate birdcalls. You might take part in "scientific" demonstrations, such as phrenological readings. By rubbing your skull, a phrenologist will determine your character traits. You might also see mind-reading sessions, fireworks, dog acts, or acrobatics. Count on witnessing one or two miraculous cures.

Strike It Rich!

If you go for the gold in California, get there first. If you're quick and smart, you could do well. Between 1849 and 1860, a half billion dollars in gold come out of the hillsides, streams, and rivers of California—that's almost $11 billion in modern money. To stake a mining claim, pile up a few rocks marking the area you want and lay your tools down. Then record your claim with local officials, pronto.

Gold! A donkey train carries gold downhill from mines in Colorado.

Lots of folks work in the streams. Just wade in, dig up some dirt, and throw it in a tin pan. Add water and swirl it around. If you're extremely lucky, after the lighter sand washes out, you'll find gold at the bottom of your pan. To support yourself, you'll need to find a few teaspoons of gold each day. Count on swirling about fifty pans of mud in a ten-hour day.

Looking for gold above ground—in sand, gravel, or rocky soil—is called placer mining. It's pretty simple. You'll need just a pick and a shovel. Looking for gold underground is trickier. You'll need to know a little about geology and explosives—and how much getaway time you have before the dynamite goes off.

Be aware that if you strike "color," others may try to jump your claim, meaning move in on your patch of land. Also watch out for tricksters who salt claims. That is, they plant a little gold in a worthless spot and convince you to buy the claim. Finally, know the difference between gold and a shiny mineral named pyrite, also called fool's gold.

Of course, many miners are quick but dumb, and they gamble away all their riches. The smart ones invest in California real estate and businesses. There's a lot of gold in the Old West, if you can find it. Besides California, good places to look are Nevada, Colorado, Arizona, Idaho, Montana, New Mexico, South Dakota, Utah, and Wyoming.

As they become more experienced, miners learn to use devices such as this sluice, or trough, to speed up the process of sifting for gold. They shovel loose gravel into the sluice filled with running water. The heavier gold bits will fall to the bottom.

HEAD 'EM OUT!

Visiting a big cattle ranch is a must. Millions of Texas longhorns roam the Great Plains after the Civil War—free for the taking. These cattle were abandoned when fighting got in the way of cattle herding. After the war, ranchers earn huge profits by rounding up the longhorns and selling them.

If you want to work as a cowboy, be ready to round up cattle, brand them, and head them to market. The job is dangerous. If you're not careful when you rope a cow, the rope could tear off your thumb. The most common cause of accidental death is being dragged by a horse.

Tech Talk

Cowboys brand, or mark, cattle to show which ranch owns them. Ranchers combine symbols and letters *(see examples below left)* to create a brand for their ranch *(see examples below right)*. Cowboys use branding irons, metal rods with symbols on one end. They heat the irons over an open fire and burn the symbols into cows' hides. When the burns heal, the animals are left with permanent marks.

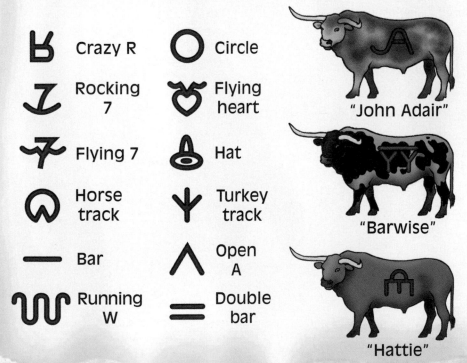

ᴚ	Crazy R	◯	Circle
⚥	Rocking 7	♡	Flying heart
⚥	Flying 7	♤	Hat
∩	Horse track	⅄	Turkey track
—	Bar	⋀	Open A
⌇	Running W	=	Double bar

"John Adair"

"Barwise"

"Hattie"

Join cowboys on the range as they round up cattle.

Cattle are edgy. Do not make any unnecessary noise, especially at night. Striking a match or rattling pans can startle the animals and make them stampede, or run out of control. This is a cowboy's greatest fear. He can easily fall and be trampled if his horse stumbles during a stampede. The best way to stop the running animals is to get ahead of them and turn the lead animals to one side, drawing the group around into a circle. Eventually, the herd will quiet down. Cowboys often sing to the animals to soothe them.

The average Old West cowboy does not look like the cowboys in the movies. First, his clothes aren't neatly ironed. And his native language may not be English. He is likely to be Mexican American, Native American, African American, Hawaiian—or even a *she*.

INDEPENDENCE DAY

Wherever you are in the West on the Fourth of July, count on a party. Emigrants often arrive at Independence Rock in Wyoming on or around the Fourth. Since this landmark is the halfway point in their journey west, there is much to celebrate. Some travelers fire guns in the air, occasionally injuring themselves or others in the process. Saner folks might drink a little punch and shout for joy.

Established towns and cities set off fireworks, hold parades, and invite well-known speakers. People everywhere recite the Declaration of Independence and sing patriotic songs. Sometimes cowboys and Native Americans stage shooting contests. Mothers sew new clothes for children, decorate straw hats, and fill picnic baskets to the top with triple-layered cream cake, roast chicken, corn, and peach cobbler.

BEES AND BARN RAISINGS

You don't need to wait for a holiday to have fun in the West. Often miles from their nearest neighbors, settlers make the most of any gathering. They hold all kinds of "bees," which are work sessions made into parties. Ladies talk and sew during quilting bees. Kids get together for spelling bees. Barn and house raisings are building sessions that combine work and fun. Plowing, chopping, and sawing competitions are always big hits with the neighbors.

If you take part in any games, you'll probably get kissed—and not necessarily by someone you like, either. The reward if you win a game? Usually a kiss. The penalty if you lose? Another kiss. Sometimes people hold kissing auctions, in which gentlemen bid on something a young woman has brought to the event, often a picnic lunch. Bid high, you win the lunch. And you get kissed by the lady.

Kids wave banners and American flags during an Independence Day parade in Idaho.

WHERE TO FIND SPORTS & RECREATION

YOU WANNA BET?

Westerners love a contest, especially when they have money riding on it. In California bull-and-bear fights are popular. People also crowd around to watch carefully refereed dogfights. Cockfights are considered great entertainment in Mexico and the West. At any moment, anywhere—among Native Americans, Mexican Americans, or emigrants from the East—a horse race can take off. When you visit a native settlement, expect to be challenged. Wrestling matches, canoe races, and ball games are especially popular.

Native Americans play a rowdy game similar to modern-day lacrosse. The game originates with Native Americans on the East Coast, but by the mid-nineteenth century, it is played by tribes in the Dakotas and Oklahoma.

Wherever you are, stay out of card games. Every loser thinks he's been cheated, and he's often right. Professional gamblers might mark the cards, slip them up their sleeves or down their socks, or move them around in the deck at will. It'll happen so fast, you won't see a thing. Once he's discovered to be a cheat, though, a pro had better be as quick on the run as he is at the game.

La Fiesta

If you're in southern California before 1850, stop off at Mariano Guadalupe Vallejo's 250,000-acre ranch. Like other wealthy landowners, he makes huge profits on meat and leather goods that come from his cattle. Wear your best clothes, and time your visit for the rodeo. It will

IMPORTANT

Safety Tip

Warning! Beware of the western
sense of humor when choosing your
horse. Never get on a horse named
Slowpoke, for example. It will almost
certainly take off like a rocket. Same
goes for Sweet Pea and Patience.

begin with a parade. Then come riding and roping competitions and lots
of music and food. Many female spectators will wear wide-ruffled, boot-
length dresses, tied at the waist with a colorful sash. The horsemen wear
formal sombreros, often embroidered with silver thread. Their saddles
have intricate leather designs, and their spurs are silver. Teams of women

*Mexican and
Mexican American
rodeos draws many
spectators. You won't
want to miss the
show.*

also display expert horseback skills, performing precise and dangerous maneuvers—sidesaddle.

EVERYBODY LOVES A STORY

All westerners love a good story. Native Americans use storytelling to pass on religious beliefs, rituals, and histories to their children. One Nez Perce story tells how Coyote put people on the earth. The story says that while Coyote was away from his home, a monster dropped from the sky and swallowed up all the animals. Coyote returned, killed the monster, and cut him into pieces. He threw the pieces all over the West, and they turned into people.

Settler parents tell stories, too. Sitting around the fire, they tell children about the exploits of folk hero Johnny Appleseed and frontiersman Davy Crockett. By the late nineteenth century, the story of John Henry, the steel-drivin' African American railroad man, is being told and sung. Some families read out loud to their children from the books of English novelist Charles Dickens. Mexican Americans may tell stories about dashing Juan Cortina or Juan Seguin, who fought for the rights of their people. Many parents tell Bible stories, which they know by heart.

Don't Miss

At Mexican American social gatherings, a boy who wishes to dance with a girl may place his hat on her head. She signals her interest by either leaving the hat in place or tossing it aside. Girls are not allowed to attend dances and parties without a chaperone, however.

WHERE TO STAY

This family dug their home into the hillside and used sod to construct the outer walls.

HEY, WHAT'S THAT SMELL?

If you're not too fussy, you'll enjoy staying in a settler's home. The level of comfort will vary, of course. If the locale has trees, your host family might live in a wooden shack. True, such flimsy homes are known to take off in a high wind, but they're cheap and easy to build. As soon as possible, the family may build a log cabin.

For extra warmth in winter, settlers cover their homes with the one thing everybody has—manure! Cow or horse, depending on preference. This versatile stuff can be piled up against the side of the house or stuffed into holes and chinks in the wood. When the smell gets really bad in spring, settlers simply remove it. At least they try.

Where wood is scarce, as it is on the Great Plains, you might be invited to stay in a dugout. These practical homes are dug underground or into the side of a hill. (Beware: grazing livestock occasionally fall through the roof.) Blocks of cut sod—soil matted together by grass roots—can be used to build a "soddie," or sod house. Some houses are a combination of the dugout and the soddie. Both kinds of houses are cool in summer and warm in winter. Their walls can be lined with canvas or plastered with clay. This lining helps keep fleas, spiders, mice, and other annoying visitors from dropping into your soup.

Hot Hint

Because it's a popular and reliable building material, sod is sometimes called Nebraska marble.

CUSTOM-BUILT HOUSING

If you stay in a Native American settlement, your accommodations will depend on the tribe's lifestyle. If the tribe moves around, they'll use tepees. If the tribe stays put, they might build large, multifamily structures called longhouses. In the Southwest, native tribes construct high-rise apartments out of adobe, or clay (*adobe* means "brick" in Spanish). These structures stay cool in hot weather and hold heat in winter. Some tribes build small, dome-shaped houses called wickiups, made of reeds, brush, and grasses. In California certain native peoples make cone-shaped houses from redwood bark. They sleep inside in a circle, like spokes in a wheel, with each person's feet pointing toward a fire in the house's center.

Native American families in the Southwest often use local plant materials to build temporary shelters called wickiups.

PUBLIC ACCOMMODATIONS

Nobody invites you for a sleepover? Try a boardinghouse. All mining towns, cow towns, and stops on the stagecoach lines have them. Don't expect any privacy, though. You'll sleep wherever you find space to lie down. If there's a bed, you will share it with others, whether you like it or not.

A good place to stay a night or two is a U.S. Army fort or post. By the 1860s and 1870s, there are hundreds of them scattered around the West. A favorite for many travelers is Fort Laramie in Wyoming. You can bed down here safely, mail a letter

IMPORTANT
Safety Tip

Do not trust strangers at a boardinghouse. If you can, roll yourself in a blanket and sleep with your eyes *open* and your hands on your money. Check yourself carefully for bedbugs in the morning.

Travelers can plan on spending a safe night at Fort Laramie, located along the Oregon Trail.

home, and stock up on supplies. But beware. Many items have to be shipped in from the East, so prices are high. One cup of sugar: $1.50.

Makeshift hotels are always available near mining strikes. Cleanliness standards are low, however. Don't bother commenting on the dirty towel. You might be told that none of the other guests who used it that week complained. Once the money from big gold strikes starts flowing into cities such as San Francisco and Denver, luxurious hotels sprout up.

SIDE TRIP TRIVIA You won't find any clock radios with snooze alarms in the Old West. Almost everybody gets up at dawn. Bedtime comes when the sun goes down. In between, it's time to work. On the trail, the day begins at 4:00 A.M., when the night guards shoot off their guns.

WHAT TO EAT

A good cook and a well-stocked chuck wagon, or portable kitchen, are essential to any cattle drive.

I'LL HAVE THIRTY-SIX QUARTER POUNDERS, PLEASE

Living or traveling in the West can mean feast or famine. During their feast days, the travelers in the Lewis and Clark expedition eat nine pounds of meat a day! That's right, thirty-six quarter pounders—each. Before the crowds arrive, there's enough wild game for everybody along the trail west. With food brought from home, such as bacon, crackers, beans, and dried apples, the emigrants sometimes eat very well. You can always count on a good meal when visiting a tribe along the Northwest Coast. They have plenty of fish.

There are no refrigerators in the Old West. So westerners dry, smoke, or salt-cure their meats to keep them from going bad. Of course, these aren't surefire processes. If you spot some fly eggs on your ham, the polite thing to do is pick them off and keep on eating. Need a snack? Pemmican is a mash made from bear oil and dried, powdered meat. If you're still hungry, try a slice of buffalo hump or beaver's tail.

...AND A GLASS OF BOILED WATER

Be careful of the water you drink to wash down that food. This is true everywhere in the West but especially along the trails. Wherever people gather, human waste can taint water sources. The water may also contain a salt called alkali. Bacteria love to breed in alkaline water. You drink the water, you get sick. It's safer to drink beer or ale, and most western-ers—even children—do so. The Chinese get sick less often, possibly because they boil their water to make tea.

SIDE TRIP TRIVIA

Six months' food for the average emigrant family of four:

Flour: 800 pounds
Bacon: 700 pounds
Beans: 200 pounds
Lard (cooking fat): 200 pounds
Dried Fruit: 100 pounds
Coffee: 75 pounds
Salt and Pepper: 25 pounds

Now Hear This

"[Thirst] was the greatest hardship of all."
—*Montana settler Pearl Price Robertson*

WHEN "GOSH" LOOKS GOOD

During their famine days, Lewis and Clark's party nearly starve and are forced to eat dogs and horses. At one point, they have nothing to eat but roots—unsalted. The more people who come west, the less food there is for everyone. Settlers kill off wild game. Hunters wipe out the buffalo. As animals disappear on the Great Plains, some native people can no longer feed their families.

Hot Hint

To cook dinner and breakfast for twelve people on the Oregon Trail, you'll need a lot of fuel—about five bushel baskets full of buffalo chips.

Emigrants also run desperately low on supplies, especially toward the end of the trip. Along the trails, a few native settlements and military posts sell food. But many travelers don't have the money to buy it. Some families live for weeks at a time eating vinegar-soaked potatoes, dried apples, or cornmeal. Children chew on twigs to try to satisfy their hunger. Adults brew a mixture of sagebrush and red mud in place of coffee.

Established settlers have more food options. But there are still lean times. Fresh milk, fruits, and vegetables are often scarce. Scurvy and other ailments caused by poor diets are common, especially in children. Pioneer mothers serve "gosh" when food supplies run low. This dish consists of breadcrumbs mixed with water, topped with minced sage and wild onion. Its name comes from what the family is sure to say when served: "Gosh! Not *this* again!"

FOODS TO TRY

- Wild peppermint ice cream—This icy delight, eaten by pioneers celebrating the Fourth of July in the Rocky Mountains, is made from snow and peppermint.

- Milk toast soup—This browned toast, soaked in hot milk and flavored with butter, is especially comforting when you're sick.

- Acorn cakes—These crunchy pan-fried cakes are made from pine nuts and ground, processed acorns sweetened with honey.

FOODS TO TRY, at your own risk

- Prickly pear cactus—The insides of a prickly pear cactus fried in lard or butter. Make sure to remove the cactus needles first!

- Chipotle (also called jalapeño)—Especially in Texas, this hot pepper is used to spice up, well, almost anything. If you do tangle with chipotle, drink some milk—fast. The milk will help cool you down.

- Critter Cakes—Crunchy pan-fried cakes made from ground-up grasshoppers (other insects may be substituted) and mixed in water and cornmeal or flour.

THE BEST BREAD IN THE WEST

You'll know you're in the West when you take your first bite of sourdough bread. Fancy San Francisco hotels serve this tangy bread to their diners. But it's so cheap and easy to make, ordinary westerners enjoy it too. Even when times are lean, you'll see it baking on the trails, in settlements, and in mining camps. To make the bread, you'll need a small amount of batter, called starter, to which you add flour and water. A good starter is a thing of value in the West. Some miners keep it in a small bottle, which they hold against their chests at night. This way the starter stays warm and ready for the next day's bread.

WHERE TO FIND SOUVENIRS

ARTS & CRAFTS—WESTERN STYLE

Arts and crafts in the West aren't just made for decoration. They are important and useful household items. If you visit the Havasupai tribe in the Southwest, watch as they weave baskets tight enough to hold water without leaking. The Pueblo people make fearsome but beautiful dolls called kachinas. They are used in a ceremony asking the dead to send a good harvest. The tribes of the Pacific Northwest honor people with

Kachina dolls made by the Pueblo Indians of the Southwest are colorfully decorated.

totem poles: wooden pillars carved with symbols, designs, and figures. A totem pole tells the story of the person it honors— like a personal website but better. You can even be buried inside your totem pole!

Many western women use scraps of cloth to make beautiful quilts. Common designs are the Mexican rose and the lone star, the symbol on the Texas flag. Following an African belief that evil moves in a straight line, black mothers sometimes sew quilts with jagged patterns, to keep their children from harm.

If you visit a settler home made from wood, you may see interesting patterns painted on the walls or floors. Common designs are diamonds, stars, squares, and triangles. Women paint the patterns, using stencils—outlines cut into flattened pieces of bark. They usually make the paint themselves, using a base of lime, linseed oil, and milk. Sometimes, settlers stencil designs all across a wooden floor, so that it appears to be carpeted.

Many settler women are experts at needlework and pass on their skills to their daughters. A pioneer girl will start her training in embroidery by making a sampler. This is a piece of cloth stretched over a wooden frame. The girl practices traditional embroidery stitches and patterns on the sampler. At first, she will embroider numbers and letters of the alphabet and later more complex designs. Some samplers record family history. They are passed on from one generation to the next.

Back TO THE FUTURE

In modern times, samplers are valued folk art. Some of them are historical documents, telling about important events such as the Mexican War or a territory becoming a state. Some samplers are displayed in museums.

SQUARE DEALS

Lots of handcrafted articles are readily available, if you have the cash— or pelts or eggs to trade. Native Americans will take your goods or money in exchange for beautiful beaded moccasins *(left),* baskets, or woven blankets. But some handcrafted articles are not for sale—they are too important to their owners.

Finger masks, made by native people of the Northwest Coast, are terrific souvenirs. These are carved wooden caps, decorated with faces, that slip onto the fingers. People wiggle the masks during dances. A Native American friendship bag is also nice. Different tribes make these handy carryalls from various materials such as corn husks or leather. They're often decorated with bright geometric or floral designs. They're called friendship bags because they're usually made to give to friends.

Settlers also have items to sell or trade. Farm families often trade homemade quilts with traveling peddlers. If you visit a sheep ranch, ask the price of a good sheepskin to keep you warm when you get home. The ranch will also sell wool yarn, dyed using the pollen or berries of plants that grow nearby.

BEST WESTERN BUYS

Cowboy boots: A typical pair sells for $7 to $15.

Stetson hat: This brand of hat, called "the Boss of the Plains," sells for $5 to $20.

Blue jeans: To complete your western look, pick up some Levi's when you're in Denver. The jeans cost $13.50 a dozen in 1874.

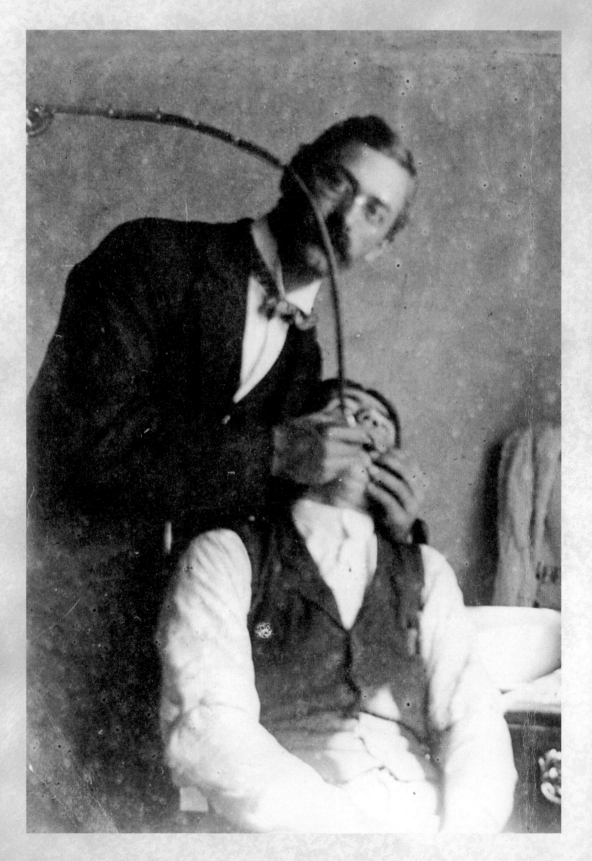

How to Stay Safe & Healthy

Chew a Newspaper and Call Me in the Morning

While traveling in the Old West, do not get sick if you can help it. You won't get much sympathy, and there's not a lot that can be done to cure you, anyway. Folks heading west along the trails bring serious illnesses with them. Cholera, typhoid, and smallpox are common and deadly. Measles and whooping cough are here too. Rocky Mountain spotted fever strikes at high altitudes. Native Americans are really hit hard, because they have no immunity, or natural protection, against most of the illnesses brought by settlers.

Unless you're in a city or a large settlement or fort, you will have trouble finding a doctor. This is not necessarily a bad thing: most people in the West who call themselves "doctors" haven't actually had any medical training. Dentists are even harder to find. If you do find one, you can be sure of the treatment. No matter what your complaint, the dentist will hold you down and yank out a tooth or two by the roots. No background music. No painkillers. Cleanliness is iffy.

Most westerners treat themselves and hope for the best. Of course, you may find some of their remedies, well, hard to swallow. For instance, to stop a nosebleed, a westerner may tell you to chew a newspaper. Have a wart you don't want? Rub it with the hand of a corpse. To treat diphtheria, commonly called putrid sore throat, eat some mashed up snails and earthworms.

Without modern pain medicines, a trip to the dentist was not a pleasant experience in the West.

77

George Catlin painted this image of a Plains Indian medicine man.

You might like the advice of the local Native American medicine man (or woman) better. If you have muscle pain or tension, a medicine man may send you to soak in a hot spring. (Warning: check the water's temperature before hopping in!) For stomach pain, he'll give you wild mint. As for the foot blisters you might have by now—if you've been walking the Oregon Trail—he'll apply a very effective paste made from the pulp of white oak.

In the Southwest, you can consult a *curandera,* a Mexican Catholic medicine woman. Known for their tenderness, these women try to heal a sick person's spirit as well as his or her body. Some curanderas specialize in attending women during childbirth.

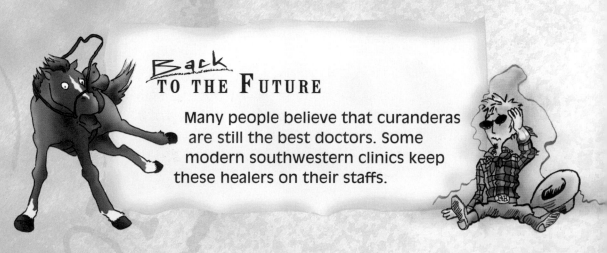

Back TO THE FUTURE

Many people believe that curanderas are still the best doctors. Some modern southwestern clinics keep these healers on their staffs.

The Chinese are also a good source of medical knowledge. If you go to San Francisco, look for a Chinese apothecary, or drugstore. There you can buy some amber to calm your nerves or ground peach pits for cold feet.

No matter how sick you get, avoid taking patent medicines. These remedies are usually packaged in bottles and often contain mysterious ingredients. Touted as "absolutely safe and effective," many of these drugs are harmful. Tired parents buy Dr. Winslow's Soothing Syrup for their babies. The label promises: "Makes 'em lay like dead 'til morning!" It's no wonder the kids quiet down: the syrup is loaded with morphine, a powerful and habit-forming drug. Dr. Hostetter's Celebrated Stomach Bitters is 44.3 percent alcohol. Not surprisingly, many people can't get enough of this medicine.

KILLER WEATHER AND OTHER HAZARDS

Be prepared for extreme weather in the West. Not only can the temperature rise above one hundred twenty degrees in summer, it can sink way below zero in winter. The wind can take anything that's not nailed down. Dust storms can choke livestock and ruin crops. Droughts can start one year and finish a farm off the next.

Winter can be especially brutal. Snow can drift so high that it covers the livestock sheds. To reach the animals, settlers have to dig tunnels through the snowdrifts. Rather than tunnel to the outhouse, some cautious settlers build them two stories high. When temperatures sink below zero, folks avoid the outhouse. They stay indoors and use a chamber pot, known as a "thundermug." To survive the cold, many people snuggle down with their dogs on winter nights.

Tech Talk

A workable, two-story outhouse relies on proper architecture. The upper-story platform must be positioned well behind and above the lower-story platform. By the way, two-story outhouses are not limited to the West.

Head for warm climates in the winter of 1886–1887. This is the winter of the "great die-up," a blizzard so terrible that thousands of cattle perish in the cold. The storm rages from the Dakotas south to Texas. In 1888 the "schoolchildren's blizzard" follows the same path. It hits so fast that in many places, children and teachers are caught between school and home. The lucky ones find shelter in barns, neighbors' homes, and even haystacks. Others die from the extreme cold.

Watch for prairie fires. You cannot outrun them. They speed across the grasslands, destroying ranches, barns, crops, and livestock. Westerners take a dim view of those who start fires. If you're caught being careless with fire, you will pay a hefty fine or even go to jail.

Some years grasshoppers come in swarms so thick that they slime up railroad tracks and stop trains. Women cover their gardens with bedsheets to protect the plants, but grasshoppers eat right through the sheets. One year the insects are so numerous that they break tree branches with their weight.

SIDE TRIP TRIVIA

In 1848 swarms of grasshoppers arrive in Utah. Farmers get some surprising help in saving their crops—seagulls from the Great Salt Lake suddenly appear and eat the bugs.

Swarms of grasshoppers plague farmers in the West.

African American men from one of the famed Buffalo Soldier cavalry regiments stand next to their horses.

ARMY LIFE

The life of a soldier is hard. Western troops are trained, housed, and paid poorly. Their jobs are many: They build and defend forts. They fight Indians. They protect stagecoaches, railroads, wagon trails, and telegraph lines. They even track down outlaws. Some soldiers do not speak English, and many cannot read. Advancement in the ranks is difficult. Desertion, alcohol use, and poor morale are major problems among the men.

At first, blacks aren't allowed to officially serve in the U.S. military. But in 1866, they are admitted into segregated, or separate, units. African American cavalrymen, known as Buffalo Soldiers, serve with distinction in the West.

KEEP YOUR HEAD LOW

Conflict is common in the Old West. As early as the 1830s, Mexican soldiers tangle with Texans who want independence. Stay out of Texas during the Mexican War years (1846–1848). In fact, stay out of the whole Southwest and southern California until the fighting is over. Watch where you go during the Civil War years (1861–1865) too. Western sympathies are split between the Union (North) and the Confederacy (South). Most of the fighting takes place east of the Mississippi River, but some battles are fought in the West.

Native American and European American forces clash in the Battle of Little Bighorn.

The conflict between settlers and Native Americans hits its peak in the 1860s and 1870s. The U.S. Army builds forts and outposts along the trails and at other hot spots where natives and settlers clash. The army and native warriors have many deadly encounters. When soldiers attempt to confine some tribes to reservations, they meet great resistance.

In 1876 the U.S. Army arrives in southeastern Montana Territory. It hopes to force the Sioux and Cheyenne Indians there onto reservations. In a valley along the Little Bighorn River, General George A. Custer swoops down on a small Indian encampment, expecting an easy victory. Instead, he encounters about two thousand Indian warriors, who have banded together to face the army in battle. In the fierce fighting that follows, Custer and more than two hundred soldiers are killed. European Americans are shocked by the defeat.

THE LONG ARM OF THE LAW

Temptation abounds in the West. Miners routinely carry gold with them or stash it close by. Stagecoaches and trains make scheduled pickups of money and gold and then transport it through vast unpopulated territory. Banks have little security. Add gamblers, bad losers, guns, and great hideouts to the mix, and you'll have outlaws galore. Don't get in their way. Same goes for whoever may be chasing them. The crime most likely to get you hanged? Horse theft. A less serious offense will get you jail time.

Western lawmen are fearless and determined. They include marshals, deputies, and sheriffs. Texas, New Mexico, and Arizona have special teams of lawmen called rangers. You don't want to be on their "wanted" lists. Even in the broad expanse of the Southwest, they will track you down and bring you to justice.

But misdeeds often occur far out of the reach of any organized system of law. Then vigilantes—a Spanish word for "watchful ones"— swing into action. These self-appointed lawmen don't wear badges, and they don't waste time on lawyers or judges. In the course of a few hours, they might pursue and capture a suspect and carry out a trial. The jury is often composed of the vigilantes themselves. Not surprisingly, the suspect is generally found guilty and, in the case of serious crimes, hanged on the spot. No appeals.

Hot Hint

The West's first vigilante hanging takes place in a California mining town on July 4, 1851. The accused is a Mexican woman named Josefa (sometimes called Pretty Juanita), accused of murder.

Now Hear This

"Dear Sir: —You are respectfully invited to attend my execution December 15, A.D. 1884, at 11 o'clock A.M. the Court House in the City of Laramie. Yours, Respectfully."

—Convicted criminal George Cooke

Who's Who in America's Old West

Jim Bridger

Mountain men like Jim Bridger make their living by trapping beavers and other animals and selling their fur. (The prime years of trapping are 1810 to 1840.) Nobody knows the West better than these men. They provide great help to expeditions and wagon trains passing through difficult territory. An orphan from St. Louis, Bridger has been in the West since age eighteen. He's probably the first white man to see the Great Salt Lake and among the first to see the future Yellowstone National Park.

One of his best-known adventures results from a tussle with a grizzly bear. The grizzly has a decided advantage and tears off a good part of Bridger's scalp. In some versions of the story, Bridger sews his scalp back on himself. In other versions, a friend does the sewing for him. Either way, like a true frontiersman, Bridger moves on without complaint. After the fur trade declines around 1840, he builds Fort Bridger (in modern-day Wyoming). The fort serves as a crucial supply point for emigrants on the Oregon Trail.

George Catlin

This self-taught portrait artist travels throughout the West in the 1830s (and again in the 1850s), observing and recording information on Native American cultures. You might catch up with him in any tribal village and watch as he paints portraits of the native people in their traditional dress. He also sketches them as they play and work. Some tribes trust him enough to let him witness secret religious ceremonies. He collects many of his sketches in a two-volume book, *Letters and Notes on the Manners, Customs, and Conditions of the North American Indian*. Published in 1841, this work is one of the most reliable sources of information from that time on America's native people.

Juan Cortina

Juan Cortina is either a hero or an outlaw. It depends on which way you look at his life. The son of a wealthy Mexican family, Cortina runs a large ranch in Texas. He manages to hold onto his land, even after the United States takes over the territory. In 1859 Cortina begins a crusade for Mexican American rights. In Brownsville, Texas, he dramatically swoops down on horseback and rescues a former employee from the abuse of a city marshal. Soon after, he returns to Brownsville with a private army, freeing Mexicans whom he believes are being jailed unfairly. On the way out of town, he executes four white Americans whose murder of Mexicans has gone unpunished. "Cortina's War" continues for many years.

Biddy Mason

Biddy Mason, a black woman and a slave, is brought west to California from Georgia. Her owner realizes that under California law, he might have to free his slaves. So he prepares to bring Biddy and her three children back to the South and sell them. To prevent the move, Biddy files a lawsuit against her owner. When he fails to appear in court, she and her children are officially free. She promptly enrolls in public school, along with her children. She becomes a nurse and eventually earns great wealth by buying and selling Los Angeles real estate. Known for her kindness to the poor, she opens her home to people of all races.

ESTHER MORRIS

An orphan in her early teens, Esther Morris supports herself as a seamstress until her marriage at age twenty-eight. In 1869 she travels west with her children to settle in the new Wyoming Territory, where her husband has opened a saloon. It is said that while hosting a tea party in her log cabin, she persuades a political candidate that women should have the right to vote. The candidate wins a seat in the Wyoming legislature and introduces a women's right-to-vote bill. The bill passes in December 1869, making Wyoming the first American territory or state to grant women the right to vote. Wyoming women also win the right to hold political office and serve on juries. In 1870 Morris becomes the nation's first female justice of the peace, replacing a judge who has resigned in protest over Wyoming granting women the right to vote. Morris dies in 1902—eighteen years before the Nineteenth Amendment is passed. It guarantees all American women the right to vote in federal elections.

SACAGAWEA

If the Lewis and Clark expedition has a Most Valuable Player, it is Sacagawea, or Bird Woman. Without the help of this teenage mother and the only female in the group, the expedition will almost certainly fail. A member of the Shoshone people, Sacagawea is kidnapped by an enemy tribe at age twelve. Four years later, along with her infant son and her son's French Canadian father, she goes with Lewis and Clark into Shoshone territory. She helps the Americans communicate with the Shoshones, convinces them that the expedition is peaceful, and persuades them to let the expedition pass unharmed across Shoshone lands. Her knowledge of trails, edible plants, and medicinal plants aids the group's survival too. In the Bitterroot Mountains, she recognizes her own brother among a Shoshone scouting party. He and the other scouts give the expedition the horses they need to get out of the mountains before winter.

Sacagawea was not paid for helping the expedition. But afterward, William Clark fulfilled a promise he had made to her out of gratitude and respect. He adopted, raised, and educated the son she had carried across the West.

SWEET MEDICINE

If you visit with the Cheyenne on the Great Plains, ask them about Sweet Medicine, their ancestor who lived long before the white Americans came. He taught his people to be brave in battle but always to seek peaceful settlements. He told them to be clean, healthy, and self-confident and to live together in harmony. He predicted the coming of the horse, which would change their lives for the better. But he also predicted the coming of people who would force unwelcome changes upon the Cheyenne. Sweet Medicine said that these newcomers would be too many to resist and that they would tear up the earth. He also said that the buffalo would disappear. In the Old West, everything that Sweet Medicine predicted comes true. The Cheyenne still tell their children of Sweet Medicine and try to live according to his teachings.

Preparing for the Trip

Make Your Own Pemmican Snacks

Pemmican is a traditional food eaten by Native Americans, but mountain men make it too. You can leave out the bear grease used in the Old West and make a modern-day pemmican snack. It is tasty, has lots of protein, doesn't spoil fast, and is easy to carry in a pouch.
You will need:

> 2 ounces beef jerky
> 4 dried apple slices
> 1 handful of another dried fruit, such as dried
>   cranberries or raisins

Using a kitchen mallet, pound the beef jerky until it is powdery. Add the dried fruit and grind the mixture into a paste. Put the mixture between two pieces of waxed paper. Run a rolling pin over the paper, flattening the mixture to about ⅛-inch thick. Without peeling off the waxed paper, move the mixture to a sunny spot. Let it dry for a day or two. When it is very dry, peel off the paper. Break the pemmican into snack-sized pieces. Put the pieces in a pouch for traveling. For longer storage, put the pieces into a plastic bag and refrigerate.

Hernando Cortés conquers Mexico for Spain. The Spanish later establish colonies and missions in the American Southeast and Southwest.
1519–1521

Ancestors of the Native Americans settle in North America.
20,000–40,000 years ago

20,000 BC   1500   1600   1800 . . .

Christopher Columbus travels from Spain to the New World, beginning an era of European exploration into North, South, and Central America.
1492

President Thomas Jefferson oversees the Louisiana Purchase. This purchase extends U.S. borders from the Mississippi River to the Rocky Mountains.
1803

Make Your Mark

Native Americans left paintings (pictographs) and carvings (petroglyphs) on rock surfaces all across the West. Some images are thought to be eleven thousand years old. But some are only as old as the Old West and depict recognizable figures and articles, such as European enemies, horses, and guns. The emigrants left their mark too. One favorite place to carve names and other information was Independence Rock near the Oregon Trail. These paintings and carvings are part of our national heritage and must not be disturbed. But that doesn't mean you can't make your own mark— or one that you think a settler or Native American might have left.

What you need:

> 1 smooth, flat rock (a river rock is best)
> acrylic paint in two colors—one dark, one light
> paintbrushes
> 1 pencil

Paint the rock with the light acrylic paint. Let it dry. Draw a design or write a message on the rock in pencil. Using the dark acrylic paint, paint along the penciled outline.

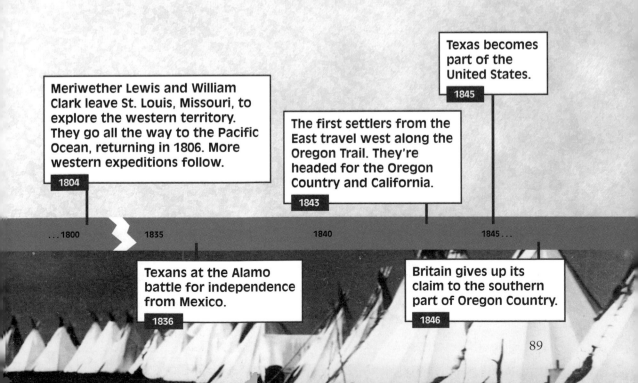

Texas becomes part of the United States.
1845

Meriwether Lewis and William Clark leave St. Louis, Missouri, to explore the western territory. They go all the way to the Pacific Ocean, returning in 1806. More western expeditions follow.
1804

The first settlers from the East travel west along the Oregon Trail. They're headed for the Oregon Country and California.
1843

... 1800   1835   1840   1845 ...

Texans at the Alamo battle for independence from Mexico.
1836

Britain gives up its claim to the southern part of Oregon Country.
1846

GLOSSARY

brand: to mark with a hot iron to designate ownership

chaperone: an adult who oversees young people at a social gathering to ensure proper behavior

convert: to cause someone to adopt a new religion

emigrant: a person who moves from one place to live in a new area or country

immunity: natural resistance to a disease

mission: a large religious complex. In the seventeenth and eighteenth centuries, the Spanish constructed numerous missions throughout the American Southwest.

missionary: a religious teacher who tries to convert others to his or her faith

patent medicine: a packaged medicine that can be sold without a prescription

reservations: areas of land set aside by the U.S. government for use by Native Americans. In the Old West, native people were often forced to live on reservations.

segregated: separated or isolated, usually by race

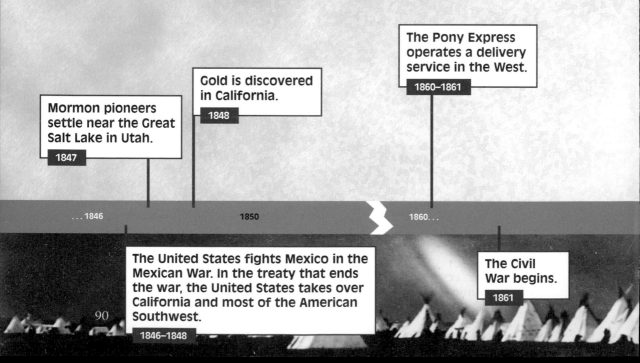

Mormon pioneers settle near the Great Salt Lake in Utah.
1847

Gold is discovered in California.
1848

The Pony Express operates a delivery service in the West.
1860–1861

...1846   1850   1860...

The United States fights Mexico in the Mexican War. In the treaty that ends the war, the United States takes over California and most of the American Southwest.
1846–1848

The Civil War begins.
1861

90

PRONUNCIATION GUIDE

adobe	ah-DOH-bee
Albuquerque	AL-bah-kur-kee
Arapaho	uh-RAH-puh-hoh
chaperjo	shah-PEHRR-hoh
curandera	koo-rahn-DAY-rah
Havasupai	hav-ah-SOOP-eye
kachina	kuh-CHEE-nuh
Kamiah	KAM-ee-eye
mantilla	mahn-TEE-yah
placer	PLAHSS-erh
real	ray-AHL
Sacagawea	sah-kah-juh-WEE-uh *or* sah-KAH-guh-wee-uh
vaquero	vah-KEH-roh

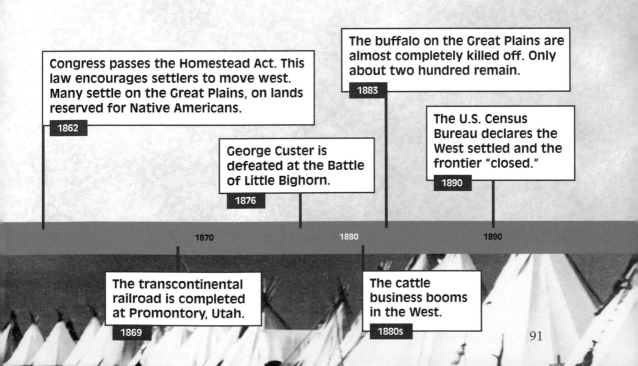

Congress passes the Homestead Act. This law encourages settlers to move west. Many settle on the Great Plains, on lands reserved for Native Americans.
1862

The buffalo on the Great Plains are almost completely killed off. Only about two hundred remain.
1883

The U.S. Census Bureau declares the West settled and the frontier "closed."
1890

George Custer is defeated at the Battle of Little Bighorn.
1876

1870   1880   1890

The transcontinental railroad is completed at Promontory, Utah.
1869

The cattle business booms in the West.
1880s

FURTHER READING

Books

Brown, Fern G. *American Indian Science.* New York: Henry Holt, 1997.

Erickson, Paul. *Daily Life in a Covered Wagon.* Washington, D.C.: The Preservation Press, 1994.

Harrison, Peter. *World of the Wild West.* New York: Anness Publishing, 2000.

Johmann, Carol A., and Elizabeth J. Rieth. *Going West!* Charlotte, VT: Williamson Publishing, 2000.

Josephson, Judith Pinkerton. *Growing Up in Pioneer America.* Minneapolis: Lerner Publications Company, 2003.

Katz, Jane B. *We Rode the Wind: Recollections of Native American Life.* Minneapolis: Runestone Press, 1995.

Katz, William Loren. *Black Women of the Old West.* New York: Atheneum, 1995.

Krohn, Katherine. *Women of the Wild West.* Minneapolis: Lerner Publications Company, 2000.

Miller, Brandon. *Buffalo Gals: Women of the Old West.* Minneapolis: Lerner Publications Company, 1995.

Sakurai, Gail. *Asian-Americans in the Old West.* New York: Children's Press, 2000.

Schlissel, Lillian. *Black Frontiers: A History of African American Heroes in the Old West.* New York: Simon & Schuster Books for Young Readers, 1995.

Stotter, Mike. *The Wild West.* New York: Kingfisher, 1997.

Van Steenwyk, Elizabeth. *Frontier Fever.* New York: Walker & Co., 1995.

Walker, Paul Robert. *True Tales of the Wild West.* Washington, D.C.: National Geographic, 2002.

Websites

End of the Oregon Trail Interpretive Center
<http://www.endoftheoregontrail.org/>
This site provides lots of information about the famous trail. Read firsthand accounts from pioneers who took the trail west.

The Gold Rush
<http://www.pbs.org/goldrush/>
This site takes a comprehensive look at the nation's biggest treasure hunt, offering facts about the gold rush, classroom activities, and lots of fun stuff just for kids.

History of the American West 1860–1920
<http://memory.loc.gov/ammem/award97/codhtml/hawphome.html>
This site presents more than thirty thousand photographs of many aspects of life in the West, including native tribes and the importance of mining.

Nativeculture.com
<www.nativeculture.com/home>
This site links to good sites on Native American history and culture. Click on the "Learn" section and find out about tribes and nations, art, and traditions.

SELECTED BIBLIOGRAPHY

Books

Anderson, Ann. *Snakeoil, Hustlers, and Hambones.* Jefferson, NC: McFarland & Co., 2000.

Bell, Marianne. *Frontier Family Life.* New York: Barnes & Noble Books, 1998.

Billington, Monroe Lee, and Roger D. Hardaway. *African Americans on the Western Frontier.* Niewot, CO: University Press of Colorado, 1998.

Duncan, Dayton. *The West.* Boston: Little, Brown and Co., 1996.

Jones, Mary Ellen. *Daily Life on the 19th-Century American Frontier.* Westport, CT: The Greenwood Press, 1998.

Lawliss, Chuck. *The Old West Sourcebook: A Traveler's Guide.* New York: Crown Trade Paperbacks, 1994.

Luchetti, Cathy. *Children of the West.* New York: W. W. Norton, 2001.

McCutcheon, Marc. *Everyday Life in the 1800s.* Cincinnati: Writer's Digest Books, 1993.

Moulton, Candy. *The Writer's Guide to Everyday Life in the Wild West.* Cincinnati: Writer's Digest Books, 1999.

Paterek, Josephine. *Encyclopedia of American Indian Costume.* New York: W. W. Norton, 1994.

Perrone, Bobette, et al. *Medicine Women, Curanderas and Women Doctors.* Norman, OK: University of Oklahoma Press, 1989.

Reedstrom, Ernest L. *Scrapbook of the American West.* Caldwell, ID: Caxton Printers, 1991.

Trinklein, Michael J. *Fantastic Facts about the Oregon Trail.* Pocatello, ID: Trinklein Publishing, 1995.

Utter, Jack. *American Indians: Answers to Today's Questions.* Lake Ann, MI: National Woodlands Publishing Co., 1993.

Ward, Geoffrey C. *The West: An Illustrated History.* Boston: Little, Brown and Co., 1996.

Wright, Mike. *What They Didn't Teach You About the Wild West.* Novato, CA: Presidio Press, 2000.

Videos

Burns, Ken, et al. *The West.* Washington, DC: The West Film Project, Inc., 1996.

Duncan, Dayton. *Lewis & Clark: The Corps of Discovery.* Washington, D.C.: The American Lives Film Project, 1997.

Websites

Farrell, Michael. *In Search of the Oregon Trail.*
<http://www.pbs.org/opb/oregontrail/> (December 9, 2001)

Idaho State University. *The Oregon Trail.*
<http://www.isu.edu/~trinmich/Oregontrail.html> (August 8, 2001)

PBS Online. *Lewis & Clark: The Corps of Discovery.*
<http://www.pbs.org/lewisandclark/native/index.html> (December 9, 2001)

INDEX

ABOUT THE AUTHOR

Rita J. Markel has written books, stories, and magazine articles for children and teens. She has also written a biography of rock legend Jimi Hendrix. A former teacher, she lives near the Oregon Trail, where it passes through southwestern Idaho.

Acknowledgments for Quoted Material: p. 9, as quoted by Cathy Luchetti, *Children of the West* (New York: W. W. Norton, 2001); p. 13, as quoted by Cathy Luchetti, *Children of the West* (New York: W. W. Norton, 2001); p. 19, as quoted by William H. Wiggins Jr., "The Emancipation of Nicodemus," *Natural History*, July/August 1998; p. 21, as quoted by Geoffrey Ward, *The West: An Illustrated History* (Boston: Little, Brown and Co., 1996); p. 29, as quoted by Mike Wright, *What They Didn't Teach You about the Wild West* (Novato, CA: Presidio Press, 2000); p. 69 as quoted by Cathy Luchetti, *Children of the West* (New York: W. W. Norton, 2001); p. 83, as quoted by Candy Moulton, *The Writer's Guide to Everyday Life in the Wild West* (Cincinnati: Writer's Digest Books, 1999).

Photo Acknowledgments
The images in this book are used with the permission of: State Historical Society of North Dakota, p. 2; Montana Historical Society, pp. 6–7, 56 (Haynes Foundation Collection); Oregon State Highway Department Photo, p. 11; The Art Archive/Bill Manns, pp. 12, 34, 40, 49, 53, 66, 68; Denver Public Library, Western History Collection, pp. 13, 27, 29, 58, 86 (top); Library of Congress, pp. 14–15 (LC-USZ62-107576), 18–19, 33 (LC-USZ62-8829), 54 (LC-USZ62-110841), 60–61 (LC-USZC4-4810), 65 (LC-USZ62-101173), 88–89, 90–91; Nebraska State Historical Society, p. 16 (top); PhotoDisc Royalty Free by Getty Images, pp. 16 (bottom), 50 (bottom); Utah State Historical Society, used by permission, all rights reserved, p. 20; © Réunion des Musées Nationaux/Art Resource, NY, p. 22; © Werner Forman/Art Resource, NY, p. 24 (top); The Art Archive/Science Museum London/The Art Archive, p. 24 (bottom); The Art Archive/Musée du Nouveau Monde La Rochelle/Dagli Orti, p. 26; The Art Archive/Bibliothéque des Arts Décoratifs Paris/Dagli Orti, p. 30; The Art Archive/Navy Historical Service Vincennes France/Dagli Orti, p. 32; The Art Archive/British Museum/Harper Collins Publishers, p. 36; © Smithsonian American Art Museum, Washington, DC/Art Resource, NY, pp. 37, 51, 78; Colorado Historical Society, p. 35 (top) (Neg. # F 28, 537), 38; Kansas State Historical Society, pp. 39 (top), 70; Sutters Fort State Historic Park, Courtesy of Niki Pahl, p. 39 (bottom); The Art Archive/The Art Archive, p. 42; Starsmore Center for Local History, Colorado Springs Pioneers Museum, p. 43; Minnesota Historical Society, pp. 76, 80; Seth Eastman, Minnesota Historical Society, p. 44; Ross Daniels, Minnesota Historical Society, p. 52; Wyoming Division of Cultural Resources, p. 45; © The Newark Museum/Art Resource, NY, p. 46; Idaho State Historical Society, pp. 48 (60-139.17), 59 (77-19.20); National Archives, p. 35 (bottom) (111-SC-85779); © Christie's Images/Corbis, pp. 50 (top), 74; The Art Archive/Dagli Orti, p. 62; Nebraska State Historical Society, Solomon D. Butcher Collection, p. 64; The Art Archive/Mireille Vautier, pp. 72–73; © Underwood and Underwood/Corbis, p. 81; The Art Archive/JFB, p. 82; © Bettmann/Corbis, p. 84; Dictionary of American Portraits, p. 85; Bryan Peterson, Legislative Media Services, Oregon, p. 86. Maps and illustration pp. 8–9, 10, 28, 57 by Laura Westlund. Cartoons by Tim Parlin.

Front cover: Ben Wittick, Courtesy of Museum of New Mexico (3083) (upper left), Mark Kayser/South Dakota Department of Tourism (lower right).